C000186690

MOTHER EARTH,
FATHER SKY

NATIVE AMERICAN WISDOM

Edited by Felicia Sarrette Wiggins

MOTHER EARTH, FATHER SKY

NATIVE AMERICAN WISDOM

Ariel Books

**Andrews McMeel
Publishing**

Kansas City

Mother Earth, Father Sky: Native American Wisdom

 For information write Andrews McMeel Publishing, an Andrews McMeel Universal company, 4520 Main Street, Kansas City, Missouri 64111.

www.andrewsmcmeel.com

ISBN: 0-7407-0073-1

Library of Congress Catalog Card Number: 99-60617

CONTENTS

INTRODUCTION

As a group, Native Americans comprise an amazing variety of cultures. According to most scholars, they arrived in what became the United States about 40,000 years ago and settled in every region from east to west, north to south. Many Native Americans believe, however, that they were created **with** the land.

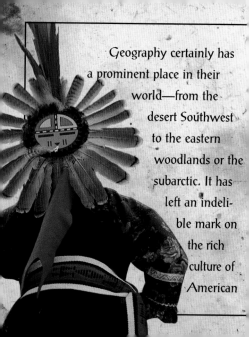

Geography certainly has a prominent place in their world—from the desert Southwest to the eastern woodlands or the subarctic. It has left an indelible mark on the rich culture of American

Indian life. The particular customs and religious beliefs of each nation or tribe further enhance this diversity. In the Southwest, for example, the **kachinas**, ancestor spirits of the Navajo, bring much-needed rains for the corn crops. In the eastern woodlands, the circling tobacco smoke maintains the bond between ancestor and present-day Tuscarora.

Even with distinct intertribal differences in cultures and beliefs, Native

Americans share similar histories of struggle and triumph. Their reverence for all living things and the land that supports this life is well known and respected the world over. So partake of the wisdom of poets, writers, historians, tribal and religious leaders, and great chieftains collected here from the centuries— the voices of those who value listening as well as speaking.

GENERATIONS,
HISTORY,
AND CULTURE

Our proud history is unequaled and unsurpassed on this Great Island. Each of us can hold his or her head high, as one of the original people of this beautiful land and say, "I am an Indian."

—John Snow, Stoney

Times change but principles don't. Times change but lands do not. Times change but our cultures and our languages remain the same.

—Oren Lyons, Onondaga

Remember your history.
To forget is to not belong.
—Charlotte A. Black Elk,
    Oglala Lakota

[H]e can stand torture and is not
afraid of death. He is no coward.
Black Hawk is an Indian.
    —Black Hawk, Sauk

We are as one
with our
ancestors and
children. We
are as one
with the land
and animals.

—Rosita Worl,
Tlingit and
Thunderbird

It was usual for the women of a household to do their own planting; but if a woman was sick or for some reason was unable to attend to her planting, she sometimes cooked a feast, to which she invited the members of her age society and asked them to plant her field for her.

—Buffalo Bird Woman, Hidatsa

You have to listen! You must keep your ear on the heartbeat of the generations!

—Muriel Miguel, Kuna/ Rappahannock

Culture is but the fine flowering of
real education, and it is the training
of the feeling, the tastes, and the
manners that makes it so.

—Minnie Kellogg, Iroquois

What we have is because someone
stood up before us. What our Seventh
Generation will have will be a conse-
quence of our actions today.

—Winona LaDuke, Anishinaabe

I have noticed that as soon as you have soldiers, the story is called history. Before their arrival, it is called myth, folktale, legend, fairy tale, oral poetry, ethnography. After the soldiers arrive, it is called history.

—Paula Gunn Allen,
Laguna Pueblo-Dakota

Good acts
done for
the love of children
become stories good
for the ears of people
from other bands;
they become as cov-
eted things, and are
placed side by side
with the stories of
war achievements.

—Assiniboine
tradition

GOOD

MOTHER

EARTH

. . . Indian country is an affectionate
term for the whole earth—the land,
mother earth, father sky, the four
grandfather winds, the grandmother
moon and her seeds that give us life.

—Karoniaktatie (Alex Jacobs), Mohawk

When the Earth Mother, your land,
is gone, you are walking towards
a slow spiritual death.

—Carrie and Mary Dann,
Western Shoshone

From the time the Indian first set foot upon this continent, he centered his life in the natural world. He is deeply invested in the earth, committed to it both in his consciousness and in his instinct. . . . Only in reference to the earth can he persist in his true identity.

—N. Scott Momaday,
Kiowa-Cherokee

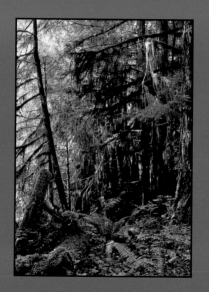

Every part of this soil is sacred in the estimation of my people. . . . Even the rocks, which seem to be dumb and dead as they swelter in the sun along the silent shore, thrill with memories of stirring events connected with the lives of my people, and the very dust upon which you now stand responds more lovingly to their footsteps than to yours, because it is rich with the blood of our ancestors and our bare feet are conscious of their sympathetic touch.

—Chief Seattle (Seathl),
Dwamish and Squamish

I was born on the prairie,
where the wind blew free
and there was nothing to break
the light of the sun.
I was born where there were no
enclosures and where everything
drew a free breath.

— Ten Bears, Yamparika Comanche

Maka ke wakan—the land is sacred. These words are at the core of our being. The land is our mother, the rivers our blood. Take our land away and we die. That is, the Indian in us dies.

—Mary Brave Bird, Lakota Sioux

Wars are fought to see who owns the land, but in the end it possesses man. Who dares say he owns it—is he not buried beneath it?

—Nino Cochise, Chiricahua Apache

Is heaven more beautiful than the country of the musk ox in summer when sometimes the mist blows over the lakes, and sometimes the water is blue, and the loons cry very often?

—Saltatha Inuit

This land is the house
we have always lived in.

—Linda Hogan, Chickasaw

Hopi earth does contain my roots and
I am, indeed, from that land. Because
the roots are there, I will find them.
But when I find them, [my father]
said, I must rebuild myself as a Hopi.

—Wendy Rose, Hopi

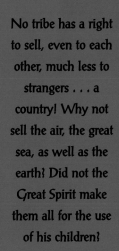

No tribe has a right
to sell, even to each
other, much less to
strangers . . . a
country! Why not
sell the air, the great
sea, as well as the
earth? Did not the
Great Spirit make
them all for the use
of his children?
—Tecumseh,
Shawnee

The American Indian is of the soil,
for the land that fashioned the
continent also fashioned the man
for his surroundings.

—Luther Standing Bear,
Lakota Sioux

[T]he Great Spirit has provided you and me an opportunity for study in nature's university—the forests, the rivers, the mountains, and the animals, which include us.

—Tatanga Mani (Walking Buffalo), Stoney

There is no climate or soil which, to
my mind, is equal to that of Arizona. . . .
I want to spend my last days there,
and be buried among those mountains.
—Geronimo, Chiricahua Apache

I have become an environmentalist
because it is over the environment
that the last of the Indian Wars
will be fought.
—Mary Brave Bird, Lakota Sioux

We're sitting on our blessed Mother Earth from which we get our strength and determination, love, and humility—all the beautiful attributes that we've been given. So turn to one another; love one another; respect one another; respect Mother Earth; respect the waters—because that's life itself.

—Phil Lane Sr., Yankton Sioux

GUIDING

SPIRITS

The inhabitant of the soul of the universe is never seen; its voice alone is heard. All we know is that it has a gentle voice, like a woman, a voice so fine and gentle that even children cannot become afraid. And what it says is: . . . "Be not afraid of the universe."

—Najgneq, Alaskan shaman

To survive, we must begin to know
sacredness. The pace which most of us
live prevents this.

—Chrystos, Menominee

Each soul must meet the
morning sun, the new, sweet earth,
and the Great Silence alone!

—Ohiyesa (Charles A. Eastman),
Wahpeton Sioux

There is one God looking down on us all. We are all children of the one God. God is listening to me. The sun, the darkness, the winds, are all listening to what we now say.

—Geronimo, Chiricahua Apache

There is nothing in natural life, in Indian life, that fears death. It is natural. It is a part of life. . . . We must realize that we all pass through. You cannot have the fear of death in front of you and have a full life.

—Gene Keluche, Wintu

For the American Indian, the
ability of all creatures to share in
the process of ongoing creation
makes all things sacred.

—Paula Gunn Allen,
Laguna Pueblo-Dakota

The growing and dying of the moon reminds us of our igno- rance, which comes and goes; but when the moon is full, it is as if the eternal light of the Great Spirit were upon the whole world.

—Black Elk, Oglala Sioux

In our under-
standing, the
Creator made
everything. . . .
And since he
made everything,
then you must
respect every-
thing.
—Oren Lyons,
Onondaga

GREAT LEADERS

THROUGH

THE AGES

Think you I am so simple not to know
it is better . . . being your friend, than
. . . being so hunted that . . . I can
neither rest, eat, nor sleep.

—Chief Powhatan (Wahunsonacock),
according to Captain John Smith, 1608

I am the mouth of my nation. When you listen to me, you listen to all the Iroquois. There is no evil in my heart. My song is the song of peace. We have had many war songs in my country, but we have thrown them all away.

—Kiosaton, Iroquois chief,
September 1645

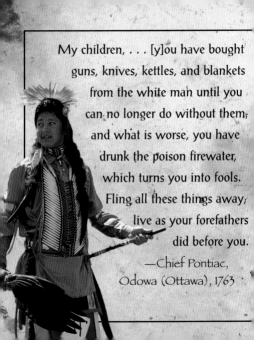

My children, . . . [y]ou have bought guns, knives, kettles, and blankets from the white man until you can no longer do without them; and what is worse, you have drunk the poison firewater, which turns you into fools. Fling all these things away; live as your forefathers did before you.

—Chief Pontiac, Odowa (Ottawa), 1763

I am the maker of my own fortune,
and Oh! that I could make that of my
Red People, and of my country as
great as the conceptions of my mind,
when I think of the spirit that
rules the universe.

—Tecumseh, Shawnee, c. 1800

We also have a religion which was given to our forefathers and has been handed down to us, their children. We worship in that way. It teaches us to be thankful for all the favors we receive, to love each other, and to be united.

—Red Jacket, Seneca, 1805

Brothers! I have listened to a great many talks from our Great Father [President Andrew Jackson]. But they always began and ended in this: "Get a little farther; you are too near me."

—Speckled Snake, Creek chief, 1829

They could not capture me except under a white flag. They cannot hold me except with a chain.

—Osceola, Seminole chief, 1838

I love the land and the buffalo and will not part with it. I want you to understand well what I say.

—Santanta, Kiowa, 1867

We do not want riches, but we want to train our children right. Riches would do us no good. We could not take them with us to the other world. We do not want riches, we want peace and love.

—Red Cloud, Oglala Sioux chief, 1870

It is a good day to fight! It is a good day to die! Strong hearts, brave hearts to the front! Weak hearts and cowards to the rear!

—Crazy Horse, 25 June 1876

God made
me an
Indian,
but not a
reservation
Indian.
—Sitting
Bull

You might as well expect rivers to run backward as that any man who was born a free man should be contented when penned up and denied liberty to go where he pleases.

—Chief Joseph, Nez Percé

Crisis changes people and turns
ordinary people into wiser
or more responsible ones.

—Wilma P. Mankiller,
Cherokee chief, 1987

We went to Geneva . . . as representatives of the indigenous people of the Western Hemisphere. . . . And the indigenous people said, "What of the rights of the natural world? Where is the seat for the Buffalo or the Eagle? Who is representing them here in this forum? Who is speaking for the waters of the earth? Who is speaking for the trees and the forests? Who is speaking

for the Fish,
for the Whales,
for the Beavers,
for our children!
—Oren Lyons,
Onondaga chief,
1990

THE WAY
OF THE WISE

A people without a history is like
wind on the buffalo grass.

—*Sioux proverb*

Each one must learn for himself the highest wisdom. It cannot be taught in words. . . . Men who work cannot dream, and wisdom comes to us in dreams.

—Smohalla, Wanapam

It is not necessary for eagles to be crows.

—Sitting Bull, Lakota Sioux

The frog does not drink up the pond in which he lives.

—Teton Sioux oral tradition

If you have one hundred people who live together, and if each one cares for the rest, there is One Mind.

—Shining Arrows, Crow

[Uncle] would always say to me, "You ought to follow the example of the **shunktokecha** [wolf]. Even when he is surprised and runs for his life, he will pause to take one more look at you before he enters his final retreat. So you must take a second look at everything you see."

—Ohiyesa (Charles A. Eastman), Santee Sioux

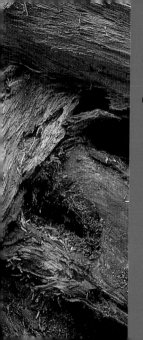

Nothing
   lives long
Only the
   earth and the
mountains.
   —White Ante-
lope, Southern
   Cheyenne

There is no chance for old fools.

—Cree proverb

Don't be afraid to cry. It will free your
mind of sorrowful thoughts.

—Don Talayesva, Hopi

The path to glory is rough, and many
gloomy hours obscure it.

—Black Hawk, Sauk

Show respect for all men,
but grovel to none.

—Tecumseh, Shawnee

Love is something that you can leave
behind you when you die.

—John (Fire) Lame Deer,
Rosebud Lakota

We do not inherit this land from our
ancestors; we borrow it
from our children.

—Haida saying

Listen or thy
tongue will
keep thee deaf.

—Native American
proverb

Dedicated to the memory of
Ingrid Washinawatok (1957–1999),
a wife, mother, and friend who gave her
life fighting for the rights of indigenous
peoples in every land.

Photographs © Steve Baker (pp. 2, 8, 18,
21, 29, 54, 59, 67, 79);
Catherine Gehm (case, pp. 6, 14-15, 22,
26, 32-33, 37, 41, 43, 44, 47, 48-9, 50,
57, 62-63, 68, 70, 74-75)

Book designed and typeset by Junie Lee